Pergamano®

ROMANTIC
CHRISTMAS CARDS

★ Pergamano® is the brand under which books and materials for the creative hobby with parchment paper are put on the market. Pergamano® is a registered trademark.

For information about products and/or courses:
Pergamano International
P.O. Box 86
1420 AB Uithoorn
The Netherlands
tel: +31(0)297 522533
fax: +31(0)297 526256
e-mail: info@pergamano.com
Internet: www.pergamano.com

COPYING INSTRUCTION

In this book it was necessary to scale down some patterns. Therefore, in some photocopiers it will not be possible to enter the required percentage. If that is the case, you can copy for an enlargement of 141% from A4 to A3. For an enlargement of 200% you also copy from A4 to A3 but then you place the copy on the glass plate and enlarge again from A4 to A3.

© 2001 Pergamano International, Uithoorn, The Netherlands
Content is used by permission of Tirion Uitgevers bv, Baarn, The Netherlands.

© 2001 Tirion Uitgevers bv, Baarn (for the dutch edition)

ISBN 90-804560-5-5
NUGI 440

Photography: Hennie Raaijmakers, St. Michielsgestel
Styling: Willemien Mommersteeg, St. Michielsgestel
Illustrations: Arja van den Heuvel, Andel
Cover design: Hans Britsemmer, Kudelstaart
Lay-out and typesetting: Cees Overvoorde, Utrecht
Printing: Drukkerij Rijser, Purmerend

CONTENTS

FOREWORD

When we were approached in February about participating in a new Christmas book, it initially seemed anachronistic to make Christmas cards in spring. At least, that was the case at first, until the 'spring' weather in March and April drove us back into our winter coats and the warmth of the fireside armchair. This year's Christmas preparations came unusually early for us. However, the topic of Christmas is particularly well suited for Parchment Craft. Christmas is the most common period for any fan of the craft to make lovely cards and send these handmade jewels to friends and family along with our dearest wishes. I would like to thank Martha for the beautiful hobby that she taught me and so many others.

Daniëlla van Bastelaere

Daniëlla van Bastelaere

I first encountered Parchment Craft at an open day in a Creativity Center in 1991. My enthusiasm for the craft led me to become a registered Pergamano teacher, a level I achieved in 1996. I have already participated a number of times in making cards for magazines in the M series. When I was asked to participate in making this Christmas book, I thought it was a wonderfully appealing idea. Because each of us has our own style and approach, this book has come to include a great deal of variety, making it suitable for both beginners and more advanced students. I hope that you will work on the cards from this book with as much pleasure as I did.

Ank Duijster

Ank Duijster

Making cards from parchment paper is a hobby that I have enjoyed for many years. It has always been a great pleasure for me, not just making the cards and pieces, but also sending and receiving the lovely cards produced by Parchment Craft, especially around Christmas time. I didn't hesitate for a moment when I was asked to participate in making this Christmas book, working with three colleagues that I value highly. I wish you all a lot of fun in working with the patterns in this Christmas book.

Gerti Hofman

Gerti Hofman

In the semi-tropical country where I was born and grew up, a white Christmas was something reserved exclusively for Christmas stories. Since then, I have been able to enjoy a real white Christmas in the Netherlands, and I still laugh in childish delight when it begins to snow. It was with that feeling of joy and passion that I worked on the cards for this Christmas book, together with three other teachers. I would like to thanks one of them in particular, my teacher Ank, for always being open to my ideas and for her boundless patience. Start making a card for a loved one quickly, and let the snow fall outside your window!

Wendy S. C. van Ooijen-Wen

Wendy van Ooijen

CHRISTMAS TREES

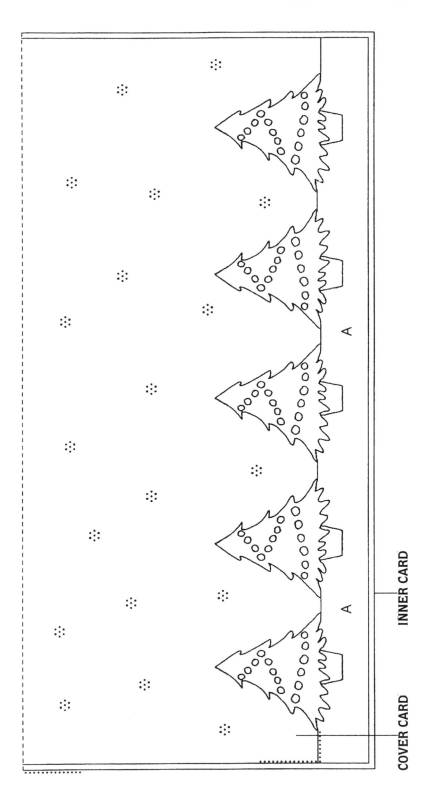

INNER CARD

COVER CARD

A

A

A

General
The outer card is made of blue Fantasy Parchment (art.no. 1476) and the inner card is made of ordinary parchment paper. The 5 Christmas trees are 3-D elements.

Tracing
Tinta gold (22T): Christmas trees, double lines of card outline; Tinta sepia (12T): Christmas pots.

Painting
Tinta Pearl sepia (12TP): Christmas pots; Tinta gold (22T): Christmas balls in trees, star shapes (on inner card, paint round dots on the Flower Tool perforations).

Perforating (shallow)
With Flower Tool perforating tool according to pattern.

Embossing
Between double lines of card outline.

Stippling
Christmas trees with 1-needle tool.

Perforating (deep)
With Flower Tool perforating tool according to pattern; with Arrow perforating tool and Easy-Grid fine mesh: underside of inner card according to pattern A.

Cutting
Cut Flower Tool perforations into stars.

Finishing
Perforate with the 2-needle tool along the outline of the outer card and the inner card; cut these perforations out (NB: both cards should be perforated and cut separately!).
Fold the outer card and the inner card. Attach the inner card to the outer card with double-sided tape. Perforate with the 2-needle tool along the outline of the 3-D elements, cut the elements out and attach them to the card with a dab of Pergakit.

CANDLES IN CHURCH WINDOW

General
The card is made of blue Fantasy Parchment and the insert sheet is made of white Fantasy Parchment (art.no. 1476). The three 3-D elements (two stars and the bottom part of the card) are made of white Fantasy Parchment.

Tracing
Tinta Pearl white (01TP): card outline, curved line; Tinta Pearl blue (02TP): candles, 3-D stars, ribbon; Tinta sepia (12T): large star; Tinta leaf green (10T): holly leaves; Tinta red (03T): berries; Tinta orange (06T): flames.

Painting
Pintura white (01) + Pintura blue (02): candles, ribbon; Pintura yellow (16) + Pintura orange (06): flames; Pintura red (03): berries; Pintura black (11): dot on berries; Pintura white (01): shiny spot on berries; Pintura yellow (16): large star; Pintura yellow (16) + Pintura green (08): holly leaves.

Painting with Perga-Liners (dry technique)
B8, B9: circles of light.

Perforating
With 4-needle tool, Semi-Circle perforating tool and Semi-Star perforating tool according to pattern; with 1-needle tool around circles of light.

Embroidering
Embroider with metallic gold thread 7 (Madeira) around circle of rays; with metallic white mother-of-pearl thread 142 7021 (Sulky) in Semi-Circle perforations.

Embossing
Candles, flames, berries, large star, holly leaves, ribbon, 3-D stars.

Cutting
Cut 4-needle perforations (corner shapes on card) into slots. Cut outer 4-needle perforations out along curved line so that the window falls out of the card.

Finishing
Apply glitter (such as Duncan Scribbles Glittering Crystal) to the white 3-D stars, the candle wax and the ribbon; allow it to dry well. Perforate with the 4-needle tool along the card outline. Fold the card. Attach the insert sheet in the card. Perforate with the 1-needle tool along the outer holes of the 4-needle perforations along the card outline and cut these perforations out. Cut out the 3-D elements and attach them with a dab of Pergakit on the card.

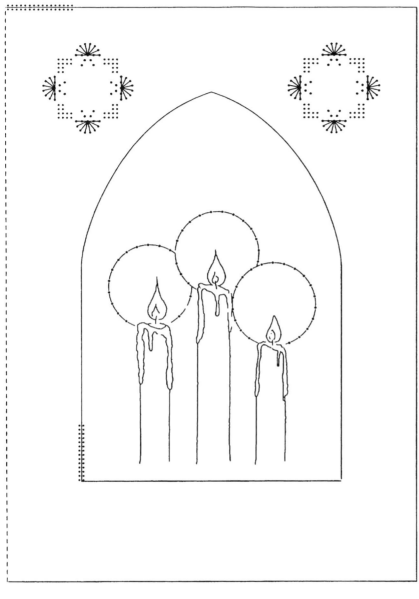

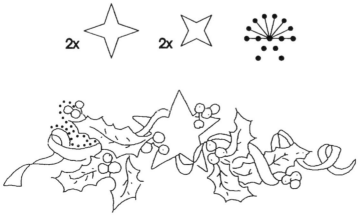

WINTER LANDSCAPE

General
The card is made of a sheet of A4 parchment paper. The insert sheet is made of blue Fantasy Parchment (art.no. 1476). The moon and holly leaves are 3-D elements.

Tracing
Tinta white (01T): landscape; Tinta Pearl blue (02TP): ribbon, curly lines; Tinta silver (21T): outline of center section, card outline, holly leaves, moon.

Painting
Tinta Pearl blue (02TP) + dab of Tinta silver (21T): ribbon; Tinta Pearl white (01TP): snowy parts of trees, roofs, foreground.

Embossing
Landscape, ribbon, holly leaves, berries. With Star Tool embossing tool according to pattern.

Stippling
With 1-needle tool between double lines of outline.

Perforating
With 2-needle tool above landscape, along outline of central section and 3-D elements.

Cutting
Cut out area above landscape. Cut out 3-D elements.

Finishing
Perforate with the 2-needle tool along the outline of the front sheet

and cut the card out along these perforations. Fold the card. Perforate on back of insert sheet with Flower Tool perforating tool according to pattern.

Attach the insert sheet in the card. Cut the back sheet to size. Attach the 3-D elements to the card with a dab of Pergakit.

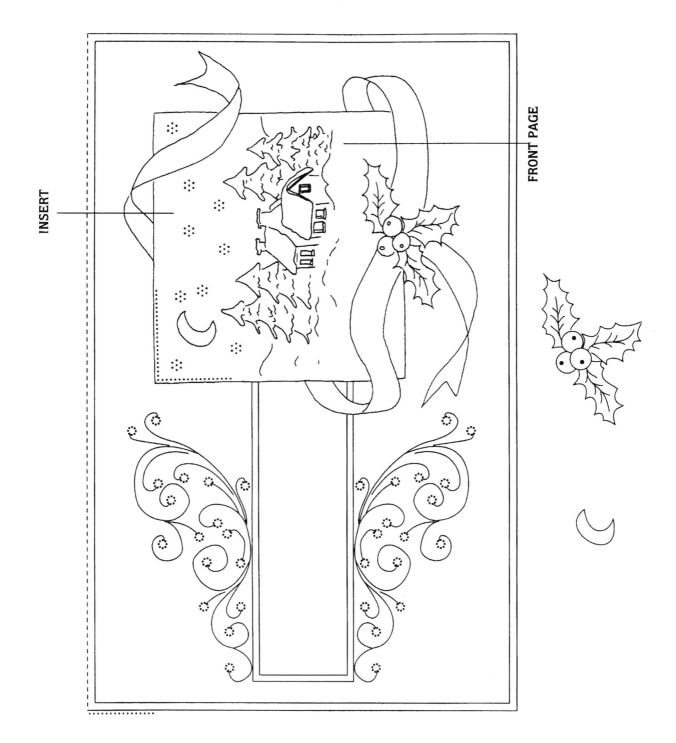

INSERT

FRONT PAGE

PEACE DOVE

General

The dove, the ribbon and the stars are 3-D elements. The card is made of ordinary parchment paper and the insert sheet is made of Pastel Rainbow parchment paper (art.no. 1484).

Tracing

Tinta green (10T): branch in beak, pine branches; Tinta sepia (12T): stars; Tinta violet (07T): ribbon; Tinta white (01T): dove; Tinta gold (22T): double lines of window, card outline.

Painting

Pintura green (08): pine branches; Tinta gold (22T): some lines in pine branches; Pinta-Perla white (01N) + dab of Pintura violet (07): dove; Pintura violet (07): eye, beak, ribbon; Tinta gold (22T) + Pinta-Perla yellow (16N): stars.

Perforating (shallow)

With 4-needle tool according to pattern.

Embossing

Stars, dove, ribbon, between double lines of outline of window, some scratches between pine needles, between perforations.

Perforating (deep)

With 4-needle tool according to pattern.

Cutting
Cut 4-needle perforations into crosses and slots.

Finishing
Perforate with the 2-needle tool along the inside of the window frames. Cut the panes in the window out along the 2-needle perforations. Fold the card. Attach the insert sheet in the card. Cut the card outline off straight. Cut out the 3-D elements and attach them to the card with a dab of Pergakit.

CHRISTMAS BASKET

General
The card is made of ivory Fantasy Parchment (art.no. 1477; size 16 x 25cm) and the back sheet is made of terracotta parchment paper (size: 17 x 26 cm). The holly leaves and the berries in the corners are 3-D elements and are made of ordinary parchment paper.

Tracing
Tinta Special Gold (30T): card outline; Tinta Pearl white (01TP): circular outline; Tinta leaf green (10T) + Tinta sepia (12T): basket; Tinta leaf green (10T): all holly leaves; Tinta orange (06T) + Tinta sepia (12T): mandarin oranges; Tinta red (03T): berries; Tinta sepia (12T): branches, bow, berries, 3-D elements.

Painting
Tinta Pearl yellow (16TP) + Tinta orange (06T) + dab of Tinta sepia (12T): mandarin oranges in basket; Tinta Pearl white (01TP) + Tinta orange (06T): mandarin oranges beside basket; Tinta Pearl yellow (16TP) + Tinta leaf green (10T) + Tinta blue (02T): holly leaves in design; Tinta Pearl red (03TP) + Tinta sepia (12T) (here and there another dab of Tinta violet (07T)): berries; Tinta Pearl yellow (16TP) + Tinta sepia (12T): space between vertical and horizontal lines of basket; Tinta Pearl yellow (16TP) + Tinta leaf green (10T) + Tinta sepia (12T): vertical lines of basket; Tinta Pearl white (01TP) + Tinta sepia (12T): horizontal lines of basket; Tinta sepia (12T): accentuate basket with fine lines; Tinta Pearl white (01TP) + Tinta Special Gold (30T): bow; Tinta Special Gold (30T): accentuate bow with fine lines (with brush) and contour line (with mapping tool).

3-D elements
Tinta Pearl yellow (16TP) + Tinta leaf green (10T) + Tinta blue (02T): holly leaves (12x); Tinta Pearl yellow (16TP) + Tinta orange (06T) + Tinta red (03T): berries (4x).

Perforating (shallow)
With Cross-Shape perforating tool according to pattern.

Embossing
Fold lines CA and CV, all holly leaves, veins of holly leaves (emboss on front), bow, 3-D berries, bottom of basket, lines of basket, dots between Cross-Shape perforations; with Hockey Stick embossing tool: mandarin oranges.

Embroidering
Embroider with metallic gold thread 7 (Madeira) according to embroidery pattern.

Finishing
Perforate with the 4-needle tool along the card outline and cut the card out along the outer edge of these 4-needle perforations. Attach the front sheet to the center of the terracotta parchment paper. Perforate with the 2-needle tool along the right half of the circular outline and through the back sheet. Cut these perforations open. Fold the card along the CV and CA fold line. The entire circular shape then appears in the center of the card. Attach the front and back sheets with embroidery thread at the center of the fold line CV. Cut out the 3-D elements and attach them to the four corners of the card with a dab of Pergakit.

CA

CA

CV

12x

4x

GREAT TITMOUSE WITH ROSE HIPS

General

This card is made of a sheet of A4 ordinary parchment paper and the insert sheet is made of Pastel Rainbow parchment paper (the red/orange shades; art.no. 1484). The bird is a 3-D element.

Tracing

Tinta leaf green (10T): leaves, stems; Tinta orange (06T): rose hips; Tinta silver (21T): outline of middle section, card outline, lines between perforations; Tinta sepia (12T): bird.

Painting

Pintura orange (06) + dab of Pintura red (03): rose hips; Pinta-Perla yellow (16N) + dab of Pintura green (08): leaves, stems; Pintura white (01) +

Pinta-Perla yellow (16N) + dab of Pintura green (08): body of bird; Pintura gray (34) + Pintura white (01): light parts of wing; Pintura gray (34) + dab of Pintura green (08): feathers of wings, tail, back; Pintura black (11): beak, head, eye, throat, breast, leg, accents in wings and tail; Pintura white (01): cheek, light spot on eye; Pintura cinnamon (52): several stripes at beginning of wing and belly.

Dorsing
Dorso yellow ocher (assort. 1): behind star designs.

Perforating (shallow)
With Semi-Star perforating tool according to pattern on back of paper.

Embossing
Leaves, rose hips, bird, lines between Semi-Star perforations.

Stippling
With 1-needle tool between double lines.

Perforating (deep)
With Semi-Star perforating tool according to pattern on back of paper.

Finishing
Fold the card. Attach the insert sheet in the card. Perforate with the 2-needle tool along the card outline and cut the card out along these perforations. Cut out the bird and attach it to the card with a dab of Pergakit.

GREAT TITMOUSE WITH CHRISTMAS BELL

General
The card is made of an A4 sheet of ordinary parchment paper.

Tracing
Tinta leaf green (10T): leaves, branches; Tinta blue (02T): berries on bell; Tinta white (01T): remaining berries; Tinta sepia (12T): bell; Tinta red (03T): ribbon; Tinta black (11T): great titmouse; Tinta gold (22T): card outline, double curved lines.

Painting
Pintura white (01): side of bird's head, areas on wings; Pintura yellow (16): bits between head and wing (base + stripe technique); mix Pintura gray (34) + Pintura yellow (16) + dab of Pintura green (08): base coat on back and wings; Pintura black (11): head (base + stripe technique), eye, beak, stripe along breast, dab of tail; Pintura gray (34): feathers on back and wings; Pinta-Perla white (01N) + dab of Pintura bordeaux (51): ribbon; Pinta-Perla white (01N) + dab of Pinta-Perla green (08N): berries; Pinta-Perla green (08N) + dab of Pintura green (08): ivy leaves; Pinta-Perla yellow (16N) + dab of Pintura green (08); long leaves; Pintura blue (02) + dab of Pintura green (08): berries on bell; Pinta-Perla bronze (30N) + Pintura cinnamon (52): bell; Pintura green (08): pine branches; Tinta gold (22T): a few lines in pine branches, veins on ivy leaves.

Dorsing
Dorso yellow ocher (assort. 1) shading to skin color: behind painted design.

Perforating
Two areas between curved lines with 2-needle tool.

Perforating (shallow)
With 5-needle tool according to pattern.

Embossing
Great titmouse, bell, leaves, branches, berries, ribbon, between double curved lines, between 5-needle perforations.

Perforating (deep)
With 5-needle tool according to pattern (swivel to left and right).

Cutting

Cut out two areas between curved lines.

Finishing

Cut out the card along the outer perforations. Fold the card and cut the back sheet off straight.

ROBINS

General
The insert sheet is made of white Fantasy Parchment (art.no. 1476). Red ribbon: 73cm long.

Tracing
Tinta leaf green (10T): leaves, branches; Tinta red (03T): berries; Tinta orange (06T): breast of birds; Tinta sepia (12T): birds; Tinta gold (22T): double outline of section, outline.

Painting
Pinta-Perla yellow (16N) + dab of Pintura green (08): leaves; Pintura red (03): berries; Tinta orange (06T): base coat on breast of birds; Pintura cinnamon (52): base coat on birds; Pintura white (01); belly of bird below, dot in eyes of birds, dots on berries; Pintura orange (06); breasts, heads; Pintura cinnamon (52): feathers, eyes, beaks, legs; Pintura brown (12): feathers, dots on berries.

TIE RIBBON IN A BOW

Dorsing
Dorso green (assort. 2): between section outline and card outline.

Perforating (shallow)
With 4-needle tool and Semi-Circle perforating tool according to pattern.

Embossing
Birds, berries, leaves.

Perforating (deep)
With 4-needle tool and Semi-Circle perforating tool according to pattern.

Cutting
Cut 4-needle perforations into crosses and slots.

Finishing
Cut the card out along the Semi-Circle perforations and 4-needle perforations. Perforate with the 2-needle tool along the part of the bird at top center and cut loose the perforations. Fold the card. Thread a red ribbon through the slots and tie a bow. Attach the insert sheet in the card. Cut the insert sheet and the back sheet of the card off straight.

CHRISTMAS TREE

General
The card is made of ordinary parchment paper and the inner card is made of red Fantasy Parchment (art.no. 1476). 3-D elements: all Christmas tree decorations, three presents, horse and five background stars are made of ordinary parchment paper. The 3-D Christmas tree is also made of ordinary parchment paper, but the back of the parchment paper is colored with Tinta green (04T).

Tracing
Tinta Special Gold (30T): outline of outer card, outline of Christmas tree on front sheet of outer card, text, text box; Tinta sepia (12T) + Tinta yellow (16T): horse, candles, stars, Christmas balls, bow on middle present; Tinta violet (07T): present on the left; Tinta red (03T) + Tinta black (11T): present in the middle; Tinta blue (02T): present on the right; Tinta red (03T): bow on present on the right.

Painting
PCE 16, PCE 17, PCE 15, PCE 10, Pintura green (08) + Pintura brown (12): fine lines on Christmas tree; PCE 7, Pintura bordeaux (51): 2 red Christmas balls; PCE 11, Pintura blue (02): 2 blue Christmas balls; PCE 3, Pintura cinnamon (52): 2 brown Christmas balls; PCE 2: yellow Christmas ball; Pinta-Perla bronze (30N): accentuate Christmas balls; Pinta-Perla white (01N): reflected shine on Christmas balls; Pinta-Perla bronze (30N) + Tinta Special Gold (30T): bows on Christmas balls; PCE 1, Pintura white (01): candles; PCE 1, PCE 7: flames; PCE 7, Pintura red (03), Tinta Special Gold (30T): middle present; PCE 1, Pintura yellow ocher (05), Tinta Special Gold (30T): bow on middle present; PCE 9, PCE 10, Pintura violet (07): present on the left; Tinta Special Gold (30T) + Tinta silver (21T): accentuate present on the left; PCE 13, Pintura blue (02): present on the right; PCE 6, Pintura fuchsia (20), Pinta-Perla white (01N), Tinta Special Gold (30T): bow on present on the right; PCE 4 + Pintura cinnamon (52): horse; PCE 3, Pintura cinnamon (52): saddle, wooden framework, wheels; Tinta Special Gold (30T): accentuate saddle; Pintura brown (12): accentuate horse, cord; Tinta Special Gold (30T), Pinta-Perla white (01N): text; Tinta silver (21T): space between double lines of text box.

Dorsing
Dorso turquoise(assort. 1): Christmas tree (on front).

Perforating (shallow)
With 4-needle tool according to pattern; with Arrow perforating tool and Easy-Grid fine mesh: 3-D Christmas tree streamer as indicated at A, 3-D background stars as indicated at B.

Embossing

Fold lines of outer and inner card, 3-D elements, design in perforation grid, dots at A, accentuate Christmas tree with fine lines. With Star Tool embossing tool: in perforation grid according to pattern.

Perforating (deep)

With 4-needle tool according to pattern.

Cutting

Cut 4-needle perforations into crosses and slots according to pattern.

Finishing

Tinta Special Gold (30T): dots on 3-D Christmas tree streamer at A and stars at B. Cut out all 3-D elements and attach the elements to the inner card with a dab of Pergakit. Perforate with the 4-needle tool along the outline of the outer card and along the outline of the Christmas tree on the front sheet of the outer card. Cut out these perforations along the outer holes of the 4-needle perforations. Fold the outer and inner cards. Attach the inner card in the outer card with metallic gold embroidery thread 7 (Madeira). Cut the inner card and the back sheet of the outer card off straight.

Enlarge 141%

INNER CARD

B

CHRISTMAS PRESENT

General

The card is made of white Fantasy Parchment (art.no. 1476); 3-D stars: red Fantasy Parchment (art.no. 1476); mouse: ordinary parchment paper. Other materials: gold glitter glue (Glitter writer), red ribbon (60 cm), paste jewel.

Tracing

Tinta gold (22T): outlines of card, lines of ribbon, stars; Tinta sepia (12T): head, legs and tail of mouse, ribbon + bow on present; Tinta leaf green (10T): present; Tinta red (03T): hat, coat, trousers; Tinta white (01T): fur trim on hat, coat, and trousers.

Painting

Pintura white (01): fur trim; Pinta-Perla red (03N) + dab of Pintura bordeaux (51): hat, coat, trousers; Pintura green (08): present; mix Tinta gold (22T) + dab of Pinta-Perla yellow (16N), mixture + dab of Pintura cinnamon (52): ribbon, bow on present; Pintura skin color (13) + dab of Pintura gray (34): head, legs, tail; Pintura black (11): eyes, eyebrows, nose, mouth, whiskers; Tinta white (01T): shiny spot on eyes and nose.

Perforating

With Four-in-a-Row perforating tool according to pattern.

Embossing

Fold lines (emboss on back!), stars (very lightly), mouse.

Stippling

Fur trim on mouse's clothing with 1-needle tool.

Cutting

Cut Four-in-a-Row perforations into slots.

Finishing

Cut the card out to size along the outline. Apply the glitter glue between the double lines of the card with an old brush. Cut out the 3-D stars. Perforate with the 2-needle tool

COVER CARD

A

Enlarge 141%

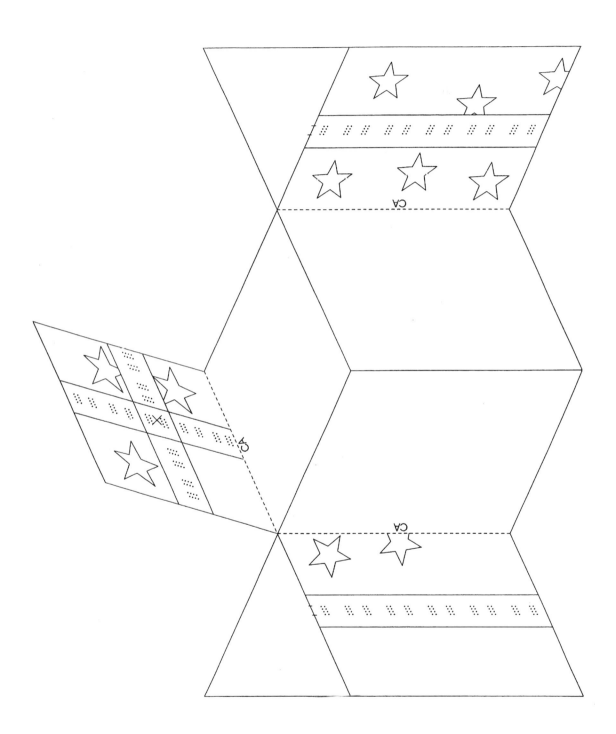

Enlarge 141%

Mouse = 100%

along the outline of the mouse with the present and cut it out along these perforations. Fold the card. Thread the ribbon through the slots and attach the ends to the back of the card with bookbinder's glue. Tie a bow on the top of the card. Attach the paste jewel to the bow of the present with bookbinder's glue. Attach the 3-D stars and the mouse with the present to the card with a dab of Pergakit.

BEAR FAMILY

General
The inner card is made of ivory Fantasy Parchment (art.no. 1477) and the outer card is made of red Fantasy Parchment (art.no. 1476).

Tracing
Tinta red (03T): ribbon, berries, chair; Tinta black (11T): dots on berries, noses, eyes; Tinta yellow (16T) + Tinta sepia (12T): bears; Tinta leaf green (10T): holly leaves, trousers and jacket of large bear; Tinta blue (02T): trousers and jacket of small bears; Tinta sepia (12T): book; Tinta gold (22T): window on front sheet; Tinta Pearl white (01TP): card outline on front sheet.

Painting
Tinta Pearl white (01TP) + dab of PCE 17 and PCE 15: trousers, jacket and necktie of large bear, holly; Tinta Pearl white (01TP) + dab of PCE 11: clothing little bears; PCE 1 + dab of Tinta Pearl sepia (12TP): heads, paws, feet; PCE 4 + dab of Tinta Pearl sepia (12TP): muzzles, soles of feet; PCE 5: mouth of large bear; PCE 19: noses, eyes; PCE 4: insides of ears; Tinta Pearl white (01TP) + dab of PCE 7: book, ribbon + bows; PCE 7: berries; PCE 7 + dab of Tinta Pearl sepia (12TP): chair; Pintura white (01): shiny spots on berries, noses and eyes, collar of large bear, T-shirt of little bear.

Perforating (shallow)
With 4-needle tool according to pattern.

Embossing
Bears, chair, book, holly leaves, berries, ribbon and bows.

Perforating (deep)
With 4-needle tool according to pattern.

Cutting
Cut all 4-needle perforations into crosses and slots.

Finishing
Perforate with the 2-needle tool along the outline of the front sheet and cut the card out along these perforations. Cut the window open with a paper knife (between double lines on top, bottom and in center of window). Emboss the fold lines on the front. Apply double-sided tape around the window (on back) and attach the inner card in the outer card. Fold the card and cut it off straight.

FRONTPAGE   **BACKPAGE**

Enlarge 141%

PICTURE FRAME

General
The card is made of ivory Fantasy Parchment (art.no. 1477).

Tracing
Tinta gold (22T): double lines, stars; Tinta sepia (12T): branches; Tinta leaf green (10T): holly leaves; Tinta red (03T): berries.

Painting with Perga-Liners
B8, A20, A19: stars; B8, B6, A15, A16, very little A3: holly leaves; B11, A12, A17, A3, A1: berries.

Perforating
With Arrow perforating tool and Easy-Grid fine mesh according to pattern.

Embossing
Stars, holly leaves, berries, between double lines, little shapes between perforations.

Stippling
With 1-needle tool between double lines.

Cutting
According to pattern A.

Finishing
Perforate with the 2-needle tool along the center part of the card and cut these perforations out. Fold the card. Perforate with the 2-needle tool along the card outline and cut out these perforations. Attach a photo behind the opening in the front sheet.

STARS

General
The insert sheet is made of Rainbow parchment paper (art.no. 1483).

Tracing
Tinta gold (22T): three ribbons, three stars, double lines of outline; Tinta red (03T): berries; Tinta leaf green (10T): holly leaves.

Painting with Perga-Liners
B11 and A12: left and right ribbon; B6, A16: center ribbon; B8, A20, A19: three stars; B11, A12, A17, A3, A1: berries; B8, B6, A20, A19 holly leaves.

Perforating
With 4-needle tool according to pattern; with Arrow perforating tool and Easy-Grid fine mesh according to pattern A.

Embroidering
Embroider with metallic gold thread color 7 (Madeira) according to embroidery pattern.

Embossing
Between double lines of outline, three stars, berries, holly leaves, dots between 4-needle perforations.

Stippling
With 1-needle tool between double lines of outline.

Cutting
Cut 4-needle perforations into crosses.

Finishing
Fold the card. Attach the insert sheet in the card with double-sided tape. Perforate with the 2-needle tool along the card outline and cut the card out along these perforations.

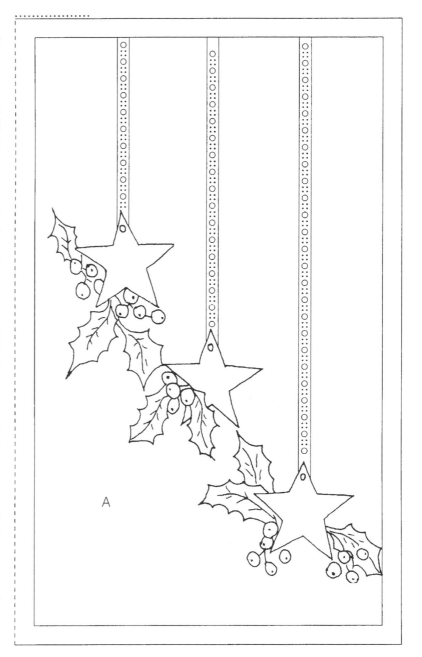

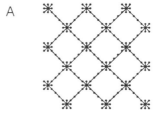

FIREPLACE

General
The card is made of light green Fantasy Parchment (art.no. 1477). There are six 3-D elements: two socks, bear, broom, bow and hearth screen.

Tracing
Tinta sepia (12T): fireplace, broom, bear, trumpet; Tinta fuchsia (20T): berries, candles; Tinta gold (22T): card outline, hearth screen, bow; Tinta leaf green (10T): holly leaves.

Painting
Pintura light green (04), Pintura green (08) and Pintura brown (12): holly leaves, pine branches; Pintura bordeaux (51): bow, berries; Pintura black (11): dot on berries, hearth screen; Pintura brown (12): broom, bear; Pintura skin color (13): muzzle, ears and legs of bear, candy; Pinta-Perla bronze (30N): trumpet; Pintura yellow (16) + Pintura red (03): fire in fireplace, candle flames; Pintura yellow (16): scarf of bear, ribbon on present, present; Pintura red (03) + Pintura green (08): socks; Pintura cinnamon (52) + dab of Pintura brown (12): fireplace; Pintura blue (02): present, scarf of bear; Pintura violet (07): bow on present, candy.

Perforating (shallow)
With Cross-Shape perforating tool according to pattern.

Embossing
Between perforations, all 3-D elements, candles, berries, fireplace.

Perforating (deep)
With Cross-Shape perforating tool according to pattern.

Embroidering
Embroider with multi-color no. 3 (Madeira) according to embroidery pattern.

Finishing
Perforate with the 2-needle tool along the outline of the 3-D elements. Cut the elements out and attach them to the card with a dab of Pergakit. Fold the card. Perforate with the 2-needle tool along the card outline and cut it out along the perforations.

TWO BELLS

General
The card and the 3-D elements are on ordinary parchment paper. The insert card is made of ivory Fantasy Parchment (art. no. 1477).

Tracing
Tinta gold (22T): wavy lines on front sheet, wavy line on insert card.

Painting
Tinta yellow (16T) + Tinta sepia (12T) + Pintura cinnamon (52): outside of bells, clappers, brown branch and two seed-buds; Tinta yellow (16T) + Tinta sepia (12T) + Pintura brown (12): inside of bells; Tinta green (04T) + Pintura cinnamon (52) + Pintura brown (12): leaves on branch; Pintura cinnamon (52) + Pintura brown (12): accents along contour line of bells, seed-buds, veins and branch; Tinta blue (02T) + Tinta sepia (12T) + Pintura green (08): blueberry leaves; Pintura blue (02) + Pintura green (08): blueberry veins and accents along contour line; Tinta blue (02T) + Tinta sepia (12T) + Pintura violet (07) + Pintura black (11): blueberries; Pintura violet (07) + Pintura black (11): contour line and dots on blueberries; Tinta yellow (16T) + Tinta sepia (12T) + Pintura green (08): holly leaves; Pintura green (08) + Pintura black (11): veins of holly leaves and contour line; Pintura bordeaux (51) + Pintura black (11): holly berries; Pintura black (11): dots on holly berries; Pintura green (08): small 3-D leaves; Pinta-Perla bronze (30N): along wavy line on insert card (thin with lots of water).

Dorsing
Dorso green (assort. 2): very lightly behind the bells; Dorso orange (assort. 2) + Dorso yellow ocher (assort. 1): very lightly above and under the bells; Dorso brown + light brown (assort. 2): space between wavy lines on the front sheet.

Perforating (shallow)
With 4-needle tool as indicated.

Embossing
Bells, seed-buds, berries, leaves and fold line. With Star Tool: little stars between the perforated slots in the border; with the Hockey Stick: along outline of insert card. With the Stylus embossing tool: accents on seed-buds.

Perforating (deep)
With 4-needle tool in perforations indicated earlier.

Stippling
With 1-needle tool along outline of insert card.

Cutting
Cut the 4-needle perforations into slots as indicated.

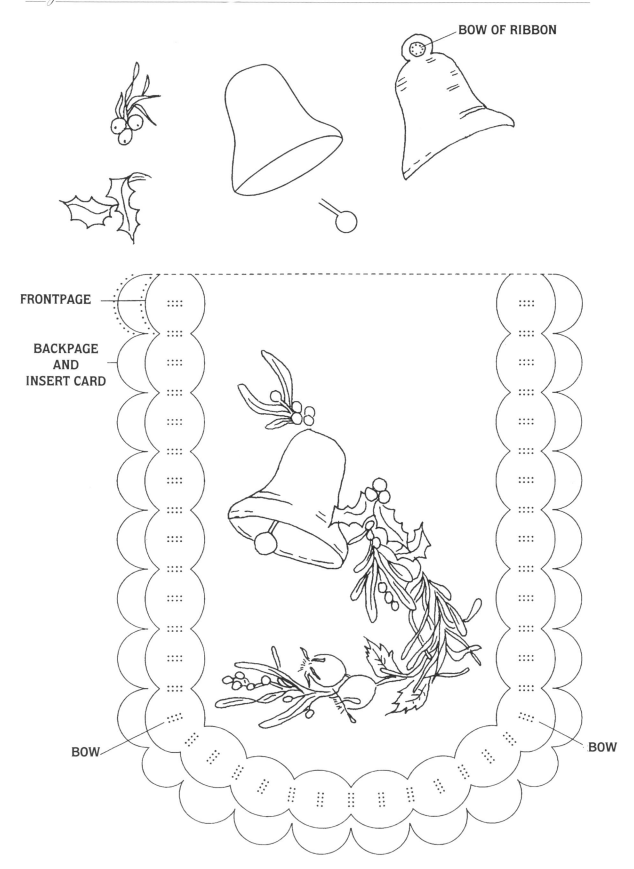

BOW OF RIBBON

FRONTPAGE

BACKPAGE
AND
INSERT CARD

BOW

BOW

Finishing
Thread bordeaux and green ribbons through the slots as shown on the photo. Tie 2 bows where the colored ribbons come together. Perforate with the 2-needle tool along the outline of the front sheet, then cut the front sheet out along the perforations. Fold the card and put the insert card in between.

Perforate with 2-needle tool through three layers along the outline; cut back sheet and insert card out along these perforations. Cut out the 3-D elements and attach them to the card with a dab of Pergakit. Cut a hole in the bell hanger, thread a gold ribbon through it and tie a bow.

JINGLE BELLS

General
The card is made of ordinary parchment paper; the insert card is made of light brown paper. The bell with Christmas decoration is a 3-D element.

Tracing
Tinta Special Gold (30T): double lines of outline, double wavy lines; Tinta gold (22T): text.

Painting
Tinta yellow (16T) + Tinta sepia (12T) + Pintura green (08): holly leaves; Pintura green (08) + Pintura black (11): veins of holly leaves, accentuate contour line; Tinta yellow (16T) + Tinta sepia (12T) + Pintura cinnamon (52): outside of bell, holly berries; Pintura brown (12): contour line of holly berries; Pintura cinnamon (52) + Pintura brown (12): inside of bell, accentuate contour line; Tinta blue (02T) + Pintura black (11): bow; Pintura blue (02) + Pintura black (11): accentuate contour line of bow; Tinta blue (02T) + Tinta sepia (12T) + Pintura light green (04): berry leaves; Pintura green (08): veins in berry leaves, accentuate contour line; Pintura bordeaux (51) + Pintura black (11): little berries; Tinta yellow (16T) + Tinta sepia (12T): base color for pine needles; Pintura light green (04) + Pintura green (08) + Pintura cinnamon (52) + Pintura brown (12): pine needles; Tinta Special Gold (30T): accentuate pine needles (with mapping tool), along contour line of bell (with brush; thin paint with lots of water); Pinta-Perla bronze (30N): space between double wavy lines.

Dorsing
Dorso green (assort. 2): behind 3-D element; Dorso brown (assort. 2): around design on card; Dorso yellow ocher (assort. 1): space between outline and double wavy line.

Perforating
With Arrow perforating tool and Easy-Grid fine mesh according to pattern A.

Embossing
Fold line, bell, bow, holly berries, leaves, little berries, pine needles.

Stippling
With 1-needle tool between double lines of outline.

Cutting
Cut crosses in the Easy-Grid pattern as indicated in the pattern.

Finishing
Fold the card. Attach the insert card to the fold of the card with a needle and a gold thread. Perforate with the 2-needle tool along the double outline and cut both the card and insert card out along these perforations. Cut out the 3-D element and attach it to the card with a dab of Pergakit.

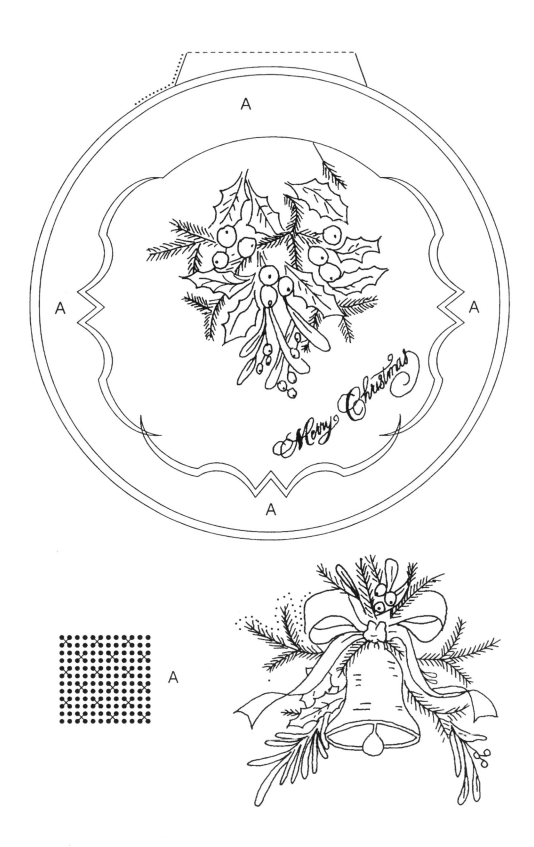

CHRISTMAS CARD WITH RIBBON

General
The insert card is made of ivory Fantasy Parchment (art.no. 1477).

Tracing
Tinta leaf green (10T): leaves, flower heart, outer flower petals of poinsettia; Tinta red (03T): inner flower petals of poinsettia, berries; Tinta yellow (16T) + Tinta sepia (12T): seed casings; Tinta Special Gold (30T): decorative line, double straight line; Tinta Pearl white (01TP): outline of insert card.

Painting
Tinta Pearl yellow (16TP) + Pintura light green (04) + Pintura cinnamon (52): little leaves; Pintura cinnamon (52): veins in little leaves; Tinta Pearl yellow (16TP) + Pintura cinnamon (52): seed casings; Pintura cinnamon (52): tips of seed casings; Pintura violet (07) veins of seed casings; Tinta Pearl white (01TP) + Pintura green (08) + Pintura blue (02): large leaves; Tinta Pearl white (01TP) + Pintura bordeaux (51): berries; Pintura black (11): dots on berries; Tinta Pearl white (01TP) + Tinta Special Gold (30T): decorative line.

Poinsettia
Tinta Pearl white (01TP) + Pintura skin color (13) + Pintura red (03): inner flower petals; Tinta Pearl white (01TP) + Pintura red (03) + Pintura green (08): some outer flower petals; Tinta Pearl white (01TP) + Pintura light green (04) + Pintura green (08): outer flower petals; Pintura bordeaux (51): veins in petals, a few contour lines; Tinta Pearl white (01TP) + Pintura light green (04): flower heart; Tinta Pearl yellow (16TP): stamen.

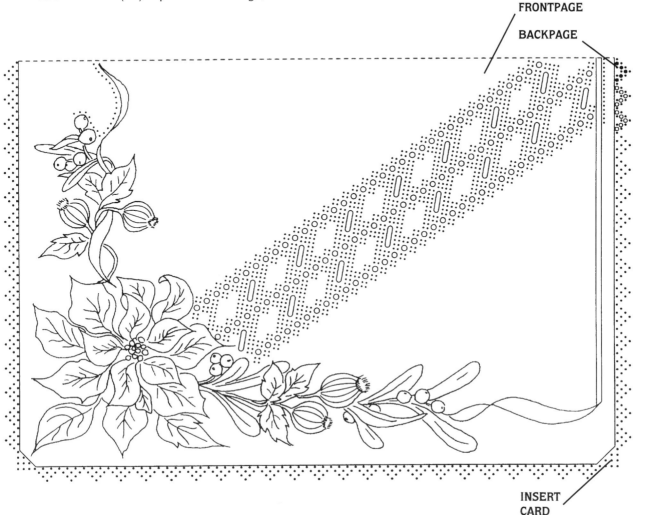

FRONTPAGE

BACKPAGE

INSERT CARD

Perforating (shallow)
With 4-needle tool and Semi-Square perforating tool according to pattern.

Embossing
Fold line of both card and insert card, flower designs, between double straight lines, dots and designs between 4-needle perforations, veins in leaves, stamen, dots between Semi-Square perforations.

Perforating (deep)
With 4-needle tool and Semi-Square perforating tool according to pattern.

Cutting
Cut 4-needle perforations into crosses and slots.

Finishing
Thread 2 ribbons (example: white/gold braided ribbons) through the slots and attach the four ends behind the front sheet with bookbinder's glue or double-sided tape. Perforate with the 2-needle tool along the double straight line and flower design. Cut the card out along the outer perforations. Fold the insert card and perforate with the 2-needle tool along the outline. Cut the insert card out along these perforations. Attach the insert card in the card with double-sided tape.

SEASON'S GREETINGS

General
The insert card and the text cards are made of Pastel Rainbow parchment paper (art.no. 1484) and the outer card is made of ordinary parchment paper.

Tracing
Tinta Special Gold (30T): outlines, border lines and text; Tinta leaf green (10T): holly leaves, ivy stems, ivy branch and leaves; Tinta yellow (16T) + Tinta sepia (12T): ivy berries; Tinta red (03T): berries; Tinta black (11T): dots on berries.

Painting (Dresden Flower Technique)
Tinta leaf green (10T): first three layers of holly leaves, stems of ivy, ivy leaves and branch; Tinta blue (02T): fourth and fifth layers of holly leaves, stems of ivy, ivy branch; Tinta red (03T): fourth and fifth layers ivy leaves, three to four layers of berries; Tinta yellow (16T): first three layers of ivy berries Tinta leaf green (10T): fourth layer of ivy berries; Tinta red (03T): fifth layer of ivy berries; Pintura green (08): accentuate contour lines and veins of holly leaves, stems of ivy, ivy leaves and branch; Pintura bordeaux (51): accentuate contour lines of berries; Pintura cinnamon (52): accentuate contour lines of ivy berries.

Perforating
With Arrow perforating tool and Easy-Grid fine mesh according to pattern A and B; on text card with Semi-Square perforating tool and Four in Four perforating tool according to pattern.

Embossing
Holly leaves, ivy leaves, berries, space between outline and border lines, ivy branch and berries, stems of ivy, designs between perforations according to pattern A, veins in holly and ivy leaves and back of text. With Star Tool embossing tool: on text card between Semi-Square and Four in Four perforations as indicated.

Cutting
Cut 4-needle perforations into crosses according to pattern A. Cut perforations open according to pattern B. Cut text card out along outer perforations.

Finishing
Fold the card. Attach the insert card in the outer card with double-sided tape. Perforate with the 2-needle tool along the card outline and cut the card out along these perforations.
Text card: dip Extra Small Ball embossing tool in

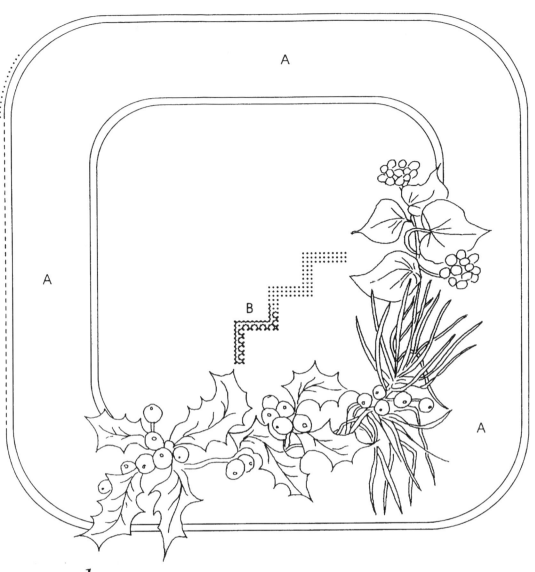

A

B

A

A

Feliz Navidad *Seasons Greetings*

Prettige Feestdagen

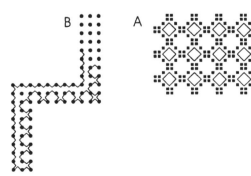

B

A

Tinta Special Gold (30T) and put dots between the Star Tool prints. Insert the lower right corner of the text card into the opening of area B. Attach the text card to the card with double-sided tape.

JOY

General

The card is made of a sheet of A4 ordinary parchment paper. 3-D elements: 10 pieces of ribbon.

Tracing

Tinta leaf green (10T): leaves, inner line of card outline; Tinta Pearl red (03TP): ribbon; Tinta red (03T):

berries; Tinta gold (22T): outer line of card outline, outline of label, circles in label; Tinta sepia (12T): letters.

Painting
Pintura skin color (13) + dab of Pintura green (08): leaves; Pinta-Perla red (03N) + dab of Pintura bordeaux (51): berries; Pintura brown (12): dot on berries; Tinta-Pearl red (03TP): ribbon; Tinta gold (22T) + dab of Pinta-Perla yellow (16N): letters.

Dorsing
Dorso green (assort. 2): between central design and card outline.

Perforating (shallow)
With 5-needle tool according to pattern.

Embossing
Between 5-needle perforations, ribbon, berries, leaves, letters.

Stippling
"JOY" label with 1-needle tool between double lines.

Perforating (deep)
With 5-needle tool (swivel to left and right) according to pattern.

Finishing
Perforate with the 2-needle tool along the window outline and cut these perforations out. Perforate with the 2-needle tool along the protruding dot in the middle of the fold line and cut these perforations open. Fold the card. Perforate with the 2-needle tool along the card outline and cut it out along these perforations. Cut and emboss the 3-D elements and attach them to the card with a dab of Pergakit.

CANDLE IN CHRISTMAS BALL

General
The card is made of a sheet of A4 ordinary parchment paper. The two flowers are 3-D elements. Ribbon length (bordeaux): 50cm.

Tracing
Tinta leaf green (10T): branches, flower heart; Tinta red (03T): flowers, candle; Tinta sepia (12T): pinecones; Tinta orange (06T): candle flame; Tinta gold (22T): outer line of card outline; Tinta Pearl white (01TP): inner line of card outline.

Painting
Tinta Pearl red (03TP): candle, flowers; Tinta Pearl yellow (16TP) + dab of Tinta red (03T): candle flame; Pintura cinnamon (52): candle wick; Pinta-Perla bronze (30N) + dab of Pintura cinnamon (52): pinecones; Pintura cinnamon (52): accents on pinecones; Pintura green (08): branches, veins on flowers, seeds in flower heart; Tinta gold (22T): outlines of flowers, dots in flower heart, some lines in branches, candle flame, outlines of candle wax.

Perforating (shallow)
With 1-needle tool and Semi-Star and Semi-Square perforating tools according to pattern.

Embossing
Between perforations according to pattern, leaves, some lines between leaves, candle, pinecones.

Perforating (deep)
With 1-needle tool and Semi-Star and Semi-Square perforating tools according to pattern.

Finishing
Fold the card. Perforate with the 2-needle tool along the card outline of the front sheet. Cut front and back sheet out along the perforations. Cut out the 3-D flowers, emboss them and attach the flowers to the card with a dab of Pergakit. Tie a ribbon in a bow and attach the ribbon to the top of the card with bookbinder's glue.

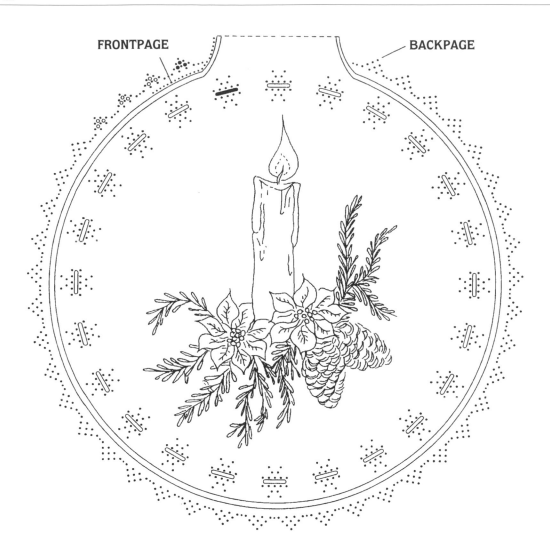

FRONTPAGE BACKPAGE

CHRISTMAS CARD WITH TREES

General
The card and the three 3-D Christmas balls with berries are made of ivory Fantasy Parchment (art.no. 1477) and the insert sheet is made of brown Fantasy Parchment (art.no. 1477).

Tracing
Tinta gold (22T): card outline of front sheet and insert sheet, entire picture on front sheet (op ivory parchment paper), note that balls of garland should be colored in completely; entire picture on insert sheet (on brown parchment paper).

Perforating (shallow)
With 3-needle tool according to pattern.

Embossing
All straight lines, inside of Christmas trees, pots and center of Christmas balls, berries, dots between 3-needle perforations and shapes around 3-needle perforations. Shadow embossing: top and bottom of Christmas balls and holly leaves. With Hockey Stick embossing tool: Christmas trees.

Stippling
With 1-needle tool pots and center of Christmas balls.

Perforating
With 2-needle tool along inside of squares.

Perforating (deep)
With 3-needle tool according to pattern.

Cutting
Cut 3-needle perforations and 2-needle perforations out along inside of squares.

Finishing
Perforate with the 3-needle tool along the card outline and emboss with Stylus embossing tool according to pattern. Cut the 3-needle perforations out along the outer edge. Fold the card and attach the insert sheet in the card with double-sided tape. Cut the insert sheet and the back sheet, about 2mm larger than the front sheet, off straight. If desired, apply some gold glitter to the balls on the garland and the dots on the Christmas balls. Cut out the 3-D Christmas balls with berries and attach them to the card with a dab of Pergakit.

FRONTPAGE

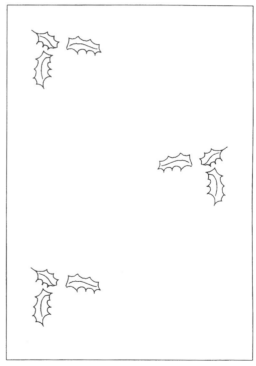

INSERT

3x

Enlarge 141%

GIFT TAG WITH TREE

General
The card is made of brown Fantasy Parchment (art.no. 1477) and the insert sheet is made of ivory Fantasy Parchment (art.no. 1477).

Tracing
Tinta gold (22T): card outline of front sheet and insert sheet, entire picture on front sheet (on ivory parchment paper), note that balls of garland should be colored in completely; entire picture on insert sheet (on brown parchment paper).

Perforating (shallow)
With 3-needle tool according to pattern.

Embossing
All straight lines, Christmas tree, pot, Christmas ball, garland, dots between 3-needle perforations, berries, line around middle of Christmas ball, shapes around 3-needle perforations. Shadow embossing: holly leaves. With Hockey Stick embossing tool: Christmas tree.

Applying shadows
With B3 pencil (brown Perga-Liners basic pencil) along center vein of holly leaves.

Stippling
With 1-needle tool pot, top and bottom part of Christmas ball.

Perforating
With 2-needle tool along inside of square.

Perforating (deep)
With 3-needle tool according to pattern.

Cutting
Cut out 3-needle perforations and 2-needle perforations along inside of square.

Finishing
Perforate with the 3-needle tool along the card outline and emboss with Stylus embossing tool according to pattern. Cut out the 3-needle perforations along the outer edge. Fold the card. First attach the insert sheet to a fawn sheet of normal paper with double-sided tape. Then attach the two sheets together in the brown card. Cut the insert sheet and the back sheet, about 2mm larger than the front sheet, off straight. If desired, apply some gold glitter to the balls on the garland and the dots on the Christmas balls.

FRONTPAGE

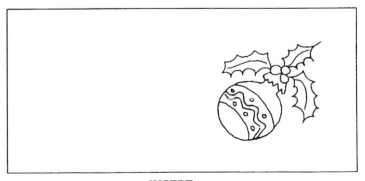

INSERT

CHRISTMAS CARD WITH BELLS

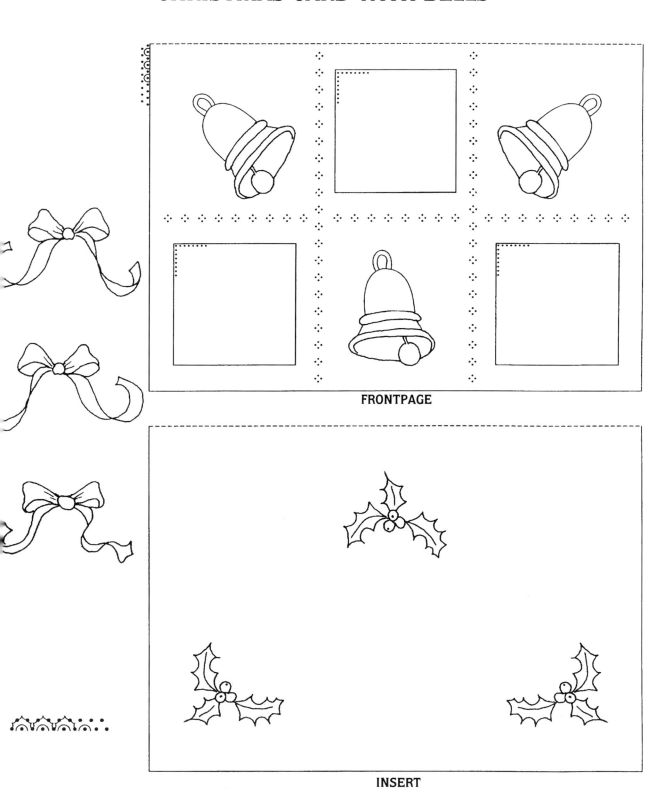

FRONTPAGE

INSERT

General

The card is made of brown Fantasy Parchment (art.no. 1477), the insert sheet and the three 3-D bows van ivory Fantasy Parchment (art.no. 1477).

Tracing

Tinta gold (22T): card outline of front sheet and insert sheet, entire picture on front sheet (on brown parchment paper), entire picture on insert sheet and three 3-D bows (on ivory parchment paper).

Perforating (shallow)

With 4-needle tool according to pattern.

Embossing

All straight lines and holly leaves. Shadow embossing: three 3-D bows, inside of bell (emboss on front) and outside of bell. Emboss all in white: berries. Emboss very lightly: clapper and strap on bell.

Applying shadows

With B3 pencil (brown basic pencil from Perga-Liners) on inside of bells.

Stippling

With 1-needle tool clapper and strap on bell.

Perforating

With 2-needle tool along inside of three squares.

Perforating (deep)

With 4-needle tool according to pattern.

Cutting

Cut 4-needle perforations into crosses. Cut out 2-needle perforations along inside of three squares. Cut out three 3-D bows.

Finishing

Perforate with the 3-needle tool along the card outline and trace semi-circles around alternating holes with Tinta gold (22T). Cut the 3-needle perforations out along the outer edge. Fold the card and attach the insert sheet with double-sided tape first to a fawn sheet of normal paper and then attach both to the card with double-sided tape. Cut the insert sheet and the back sheet, about 2mm larger than the front sheet, off straight. Attach the three 3-D bows to the bells with a dab of Pergakit.

GIFT TAG WITH BELL

General

The card is made of ivory Fantasy Parchment (art.no. 1477), the insert sheet and the 3-D bow are made of brown Fantasy Parchment (art.no. 1477).

Tracing

Tinta gold (22T): card outline of front sheet and insert sheet, entire picture on front sheet (on ivory parchment paper) and entire picture on insert sheet and 3-D bow (on brown parchment paper).

Perforating (shallow)

With 4-needle tool according to pattern.

Embossing

All straight lines and holly leaves. Shadow embossing: 3-D bow, inside of bell (emboss on front shadow) and outside of bell. Emboss as white as possible: berries and dots between 4-needle perforations. Emboss very lightly: clapper and band on bell.

Applying shadows

With B3 pencil (brown basic pencil from Perga-Liners) on inside of bell.

Stippling

With 1-needle tool clapper and strap on bell.

Perforating

With 2-needle tool along inside of square.

Perforating (deep)

With 4-needle tool according to pattern.

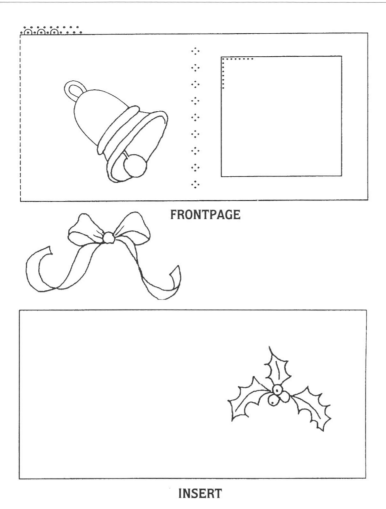

FRONTPAGE

INSERT

Cutting

Cut out 2-needle perforations along inside of square. Cut out 3-D bow.

Finishing

Perforate with the 3-needle tool along the card outline and trace semi-circles around alternating holes with Tinta gold (22T). Cut out the 3-needle perforations along the outer edge. Fold the card and attach the brown insert sheet in the card with double-sided tape. Cut the insert sheet and the back sheet, about 2mm larger than the front sheet, off straight. Attach the 3-D bow to the bell with a dab of Pergakit.

SLEIGH WITH PACKAGES

General

The card contains an insert sheet made of ordinary parchment paper that is the same size as the front sheet; the picture is painted on this. An insert sheet the same size as the back sheet, made of Rainbow parchment paper Pastel (art.no. 1484), is attached under it.

Tracing

Tinta black (11T): entire picture, card outline, stars, outline of frame; Tinta gold (22T): card outline and frame a second time, flat along black line.

Painting with Perga Colors Exclusive

PCE 1, PCE 2: alternate stars; PCE 2: bear; PCE 3: muzzle of bear; PCE 14: scarf of bear; PCE 7: pillow under bear, staff, nose and doll's clothing; PCE 14, PCE 13: top package behind bear; PCE 1: doll's hair, center package behind bear; PCE 6: bottom package behind bear; PCE 3, PCE 19: bag, rope, sleigh; PCE 11, PCE 14: book in bag; PCE 16, PCE 7:

FRONTPAGE

INSERT

long package in the bag; PCE 4: doll's face; PCE 5, PCE 6, PCE 11: package at back of sleigh; PCE 11: all bows.

Dorsing
Dorso blue (assort. 1): sky.

Perforating (shallow)
With 5-needle tool according to pattern.

Embossing
Stars, sleigh, bear, all packages, doll, bag, snowflakes on background, between 5 needle perforations according to pattern; with Hockey Stick embossing tool: snow under sleigh.

Stippling
With 1-needle tool the snow on the ground.

Perforating (deep)
With 5-needle tool in previous 5-needle perforations. Swivel gently from left to right.

Finishing
Perforate with the 2-needle tool along the frame and cut out these perforations so the window falls out. Attach the insert sheet with the picture to the insert sheet of Pastel Rainbow parchment paper with double-sided tape. Fold the card and attach both insert sheets with double-sided tape. Cut out the 5-needle perforations along the outer edge and cut the insert sheets and the back sheet off straight.

CHRISTMAS STORIES

General
The card is made of blue Fantasy Parchment and the oval 3-D element is made of white Fantasy Parchment (art.no. 1476). The 3-D Christmas design is made of ordinary parchment paper.

Blue card
Printing (on front)
Dip Star Tool embossing tool in Tinta Special Gold (30T) and use it to print stars on top half of card according to pattern. Dip Extra Small Ball embossing tool in Tinta Pearl white (01TP) and use it to print dots on bottom half of card according to pattern.

Embossing
With Star Tool embossing tool around the dots (on back); the silver dots (on back) with Extra Small Ball embossing tool.

3-D element (oval)
Tracing
Tinta Special Gold (30T): border of oval; mixture of Tinta black (11T) 40% + Tinta blue (02T) 10% + water 50%: entire design.

Painting
Tinta Special Gold (30T): coat buttons; Tinta Pearl yellow (16TP) + Tinta sepia (12T): buttons on front of armrest; with PCE (Perga Colors Exclusive): rest of design (according to pattern).

Perforating (shallow)
With Semi-Circle perforating tool according to pattern.

Embossing
Lines in Semi-Circle perforations, eyes, nose and buttons. With Hockey Stick embossing tool: rest of design.

Perforating (deep)
With Semi-Circle perforating tool according to pattern.

Cutting
Cut out 3-D element along Semi-Circle perforations.

Finishing
Trace the spine of the book with Tinta Special Gold (30T).

3-D element (Christmas design)
Tracing
With Tinta silver (21T): entire design.

Painting
With PCE according to pattern.

Embossing
Entire Christmas design.

Finishing off (general)
Fold the card and cut it off straight. Cut out the 3-D elements and attach them to the card with a dab of Pergakit.

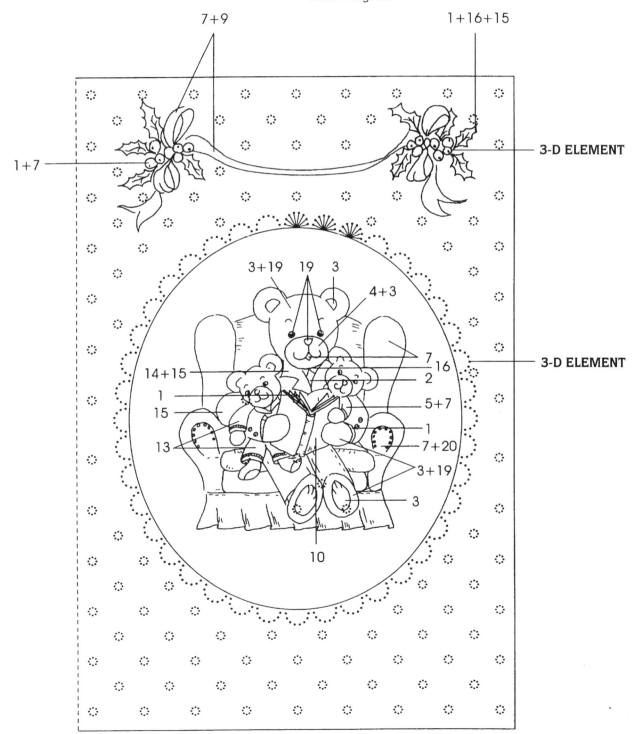

MUSICAL BEARS

General
The card contains an insert sheet of ordinary parchment paper.

Tracing
Tinta white (01T): double straight lines, double curved lines, snowflakes, snow on trees and ground, white edges on coat of bear in back; Tinta leaf green (10T): green of trees; Tinta sepia (12T): tree trunks, two bears, trumpet, drumsticks and drum strap; Tinta black (11T): nose and eyes of bear in front; Tinta blue (02T): trousers and scarves of two bears;

Tinta turquoise (05T): sweater and tassels on scarf of bear in front; Tinta red (03T): drum and jacket of bear in back.

Painting with Perga-Liners
B1, A1 and A2: snow on trees; B1 and A1: white edges on coat of bear in back; B7, B6, A15 and A16: green of trees and surfaces of drum; B3 and A17: nose of bear in back, tree trunks and brown parts of bear in front; B10 and A10: inside of ears of both bears; B8, A19 and A18: muzzle of bear in front, drumhead and bear in back; B1, B5, A1 and

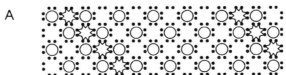

A7: scarf of bear in front; B1 and A6: blouse of bear in front; B8, A20 and A11: drumsticks; B11 and A12: edges of drum; B8 and A20: drum strap; B1, B5, A1, A7 and a bit of A4: trousers of bear in front; B1, B4, A1 and A4: scarf and trousers of bear in back; B1, B11, A1 and A12: jacket of bear in back; B2 and A3: eyes and nose of bear in front; B3, A17 and A3: eyes of bear in back; B8, A20, A11 and a bit of A17: trumpet; A2: bit of a shadow in snow.

Dorsing

Dorso blue (assort.1): sky; Dorso yellow (assort. 1) and Dorso orange (assort. 2): sun.

Perforating

With Easy-Grid fine mesh and Arrow perforating tool: in border between straight double lines and double curved lines according to pattern.

Embossing

Drum, drumsticks, trumpet, snowflakes and dots between Easy-Grid perforations. Emboss very lightly: between all double lines. With Hockey Stick embossing tool: snow on ground; with Hockey Stick embossing tool and Extra Large Ball embossing tool: bears and trees.

Stippling

With 1-needle tool between double curved lines.

Cutting

Cut the stars in the border out diagonally with Easy-Grid perforations (see color example).

Finishing

Fold the card. Use a sheet of parchment paper as an insert sheet. Trace the inner straight outline and the outer curved line with Tinta white (01T). Dorse between the two lines with Dorso blue (assort. 1). Attach the insert sheet in the card with double-sided tape. Perforate with the 2-needle tool along the card outline and cut it out along the perforations.

CHURCH IN WINTER LANDSCAPE

General

The card consists of six parts: 2 x outer border and 2 x inner sections of ordinary parchment paper, 1 x insert sheet for outer edge made of red Fantasy Parchment (art.no. 1476) and 1 x insert sheet for inner section made of white Fantasy Parchment (art.no. 1476). The outer border and the inner section are done the same way twice.

Tracing

Tinta white (01T): all lines of outer border; Tinta Special Gold (30T): outline of inner section; Tinta Pearl white (01TP): snow, mountains, roofs, trees and snow on top of garden gates; Tinta sepia (12T): contour lines of church, windows and garden gates.

Painting

Paint with Perga Colors Exclusive by the numbers in the pattern.
Tinta Special Gold (30T): dots between Star Tool designs.

Dorsing

Dorso lilac (assort. 2), Dorso yellow (assort. 1), Dorso blue (assort. 1), Dorso black (assort. 2): behind mountains and sky (from top to bottom).

Embossing

With Star Tool embossing tool according to pattern; with Hockey Stick embossing tool: snow, mountains, tower, roofs, trees and garden gates. Space between double lines of outer border.

Stippling

With 1-needle tool space between double lines of outer border.

Perforating

With 2-needle tool areas between curved lines in outer border, along outlines of outer border and along outline of inner section.

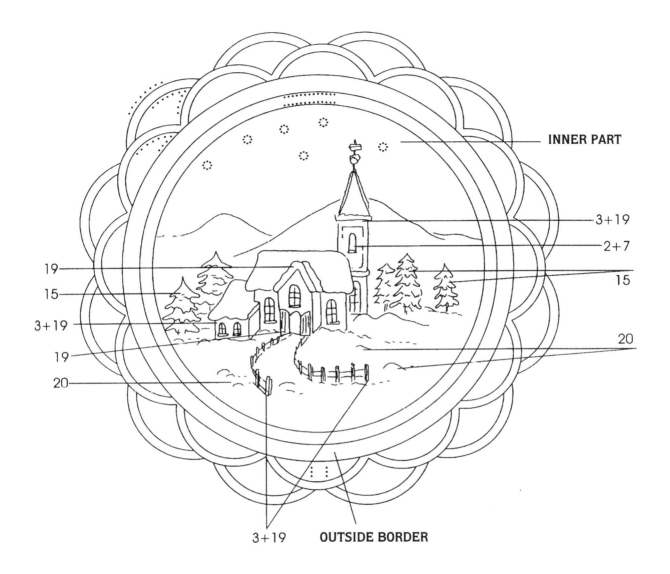

INNER PART

3+19

2+7

15

20

19

15

3+19

19

20

3+19   **OUTSIDE BORDER**

Cutting

Cut out areas between curved lines, outer edge and inner section along 2-needle perforation.

Finishing

Cut out the white and red insert sheets along the outline. Attach the red insert sheet between both parts of the outer border, and attach the white insert sheet between both parts of the inner section (use double-sided tape or pieces of foam tape). Attach a gold thread between the inner section and the outer border. With the 2-needle tool, perforate two slots at the bottom of the outer border and cut them open. Then thread two ribbons (each about 20 cm long, for example red and gold intertwined) through the openings and tie a bow from both ends.

CHRISTMAS BALL

General

All elements (holly leaves, berries, border and Christmas ball) are 3-D elements. The Christmas ball is traced on red Fantasy Parchment (art.no. 1476).

Tracing

Tinta gold (22T): card outline, Christmas ball, star in Christmas ball, border with ribbon; Tinta white (01T): star shapes in border; if desired: Tinta leaf green (10T): holly leaves; Tinta fuchsia (20T): berries.

BACKPAGE

FRONTPAGE

Painting

Pintura yellow (16), Pintura light green (04), Pintura green (08) and Pintura brown (12): holly leaves; Pintura bordeaux (51): berries; Pintura black (11): dots and shadows in berries; Pintura white (01): shiny spots in berries.

Perforating (shallow)

With 4-needle tool, Semi-Circle perforating tool and Semi-Star according to pattern.

Embossing

Between perforations in section and card border on front sheet, berries, outside star in Christmas ball. With Hockey Stick embossing tool: holly leaves (highlights along veins).

Stippling

With 1-needle tool ribbon and inside star in Christmas ball.

Perforating (deep)

With 4-needle tool according to pattern. With Flower Tool perforating tool and 1-needle tool: perforations around star shapes in border.

Cutting

Cut all 4-needle perforations into crosses and slots.

Embroidering

Embroider with metallic gold thread 7 (Madeira) according to embroidery pattern.

Finishing

Fold the card. Perforate with the 4-needle tool along the outline of the back sheet and cut the card out along the outer perforations. Also cut out the outer 4-needle perforations on the front sheet. Perforate along the 3-D elements with the 2-needle tool. Cut the 3-D elements out and attach them to the card with a dab of Pergakit. Attach a separate border made of red Fantasy Parchment under the border.

CHRISTMAS BELLS

General

The outer card is made of white Fantasy Parchment and the inner card is made of red Fantasy Parchment (art.no. 1476).

Tracing

Tinta gold (22T): card outline of outer card, double lines of wreath, stars, if desired: Christmas bells; Tinta red (03T): ribbon; Tinta white (01T): shapes in corners, berries; Tinta leaf green (10T): pine branch, leaves.

Painting

Pintura brown (12) + Pinta-Perla bronze (30N): Christmas bells; Pintura brown (12): clappers; Pintura light green (04) + Pintura green (08) + dab of Pintura brown (12): pine branch, leaves; Pintura white (01) + dab of Pintura light green (04): berries; Pintura black (11): dot on berries; Pintura red (03) + Pintura bordeaux (51) + dab of Pintura black (11): ribbon.

Perforating (shallow)

With 5-needle tool and Semi-Circle perforating tool according to pattern.

Embossing

On front: inside of bells; on back: clappers, bells (lightly), star shapes, double lines of wreath, between 5-needle perforations according to pattern, berries, ribbon, shapes in corners.

Perforating (deep)

With 5-needle tool and Semi-Circle perforating tool according to pattern. NB: go back to 5-needle perforations along card outline and swivel slightly to left and right!

Embroidering

Embroider with metallic gold thread 7 (Madeira) according to embroidery pattern.

58

Finishing off

Fold the inner card. Perforate with the 2-needle tool along the outline of the inner card and cut the card out along these perforations. Perforate with the 2-needle tool along the outline of the outer card according to pattern. Cut out the front sheet of the outer card along the 2-needle perforations and the outer 5-needle perforations. Fold the outer card and cut the back sheet off straight. Attach the inner card in the outer card with double-sided tape.

COVER CARD

INNER CARD

SNOWMAN AND MICE

General

The card consists of an inner card made of white marbled parchment paper and an outer card made of ordinary parchment paper. 3-D elements: snowman (head and body, 2 arms), hat, snow on edge of hat, top part of scarf, nose, bird.

Tracing

Tinta black (11T): hat, eyes, mouth, buttons, mice; Tinta orange (06T): scarf, nose; Tinta turquoise (05T): snowman, lines around eyes, snow on edge of hat, bottom part, snowballs; Tinta silver (21T): lines between perforations, border, outline of outer card.

Painting

Pintura white (01) + dab of Pinta-Perla blue (02N): snowman, snowballs, snow on bottom part; Pintura black (11): eyes, mouth, buttons, hat; Pintura orange (06): nose, scarf, 2 lines on hat; Pintura green (08): stripes on scarf, fringe; Pintura skin color (13) + dab of Pintura gray (34): mice; Tinta silver (21T): trace mice; Pintura cinnamon (52): bird; Pintura brown (12): accentuate bird; Pintura orange (06): beak.

Dorsing

Dorso orange (assort. 2): front sheet of outer card; Dorso light blue (assort. 2): behind snowman.

Perforating (shallow)

With 5-needle tool and Semi-Star perforating tool according to pattern.

Embossing
3-D elements, foreground of snow, mice, between 5-needle perforations.

Perforating (deep)
With 5-needle tool (swivel to left and right) and Semi-Star perforating tool according to pattern.

Finishing
Perforate with the 2-needle tool along the window of the card and along the 3-D elements. Cut these perforations out. Fold the inner and outer card. Attach the inner card in the outer card with double-sided tape and cut the cards off straight. Attach all 3-D elements to the inner card with a dab of Pergakit.

SNOWMAN ON SLED

General
This card contains an insert sheet made of ordinary parchment paper on which the opening onto a snowy landscape can be seen.

Tracing
Insert sheet:
Tinta white (01T): snow on ground, trees and roof; Tinta blue (02T): window frames; Tinta sepia (12T): house; Tinta leaf green (10T): trees and doors.

Front sheet:
Tinta white (01T): snowman, edge and pom-pom on hat; Tinta red (03T): hat, red parts of scarf and present; Tinta blue (02T): double lines of outline, line around opening, bow, blue parts of scarf; Tinta sepia (12T): stones of mouth, sleigh and rope; Tinta orange (06T): nose; Tinta black (11T): eyes.

Painting with Perga-Liners
B1, A1 and a bit of A2: snowman and snow on landscape; B1, B11, A1 and A12: hat; B1, B5, A1, A6 and A7: edge and pom-pom of hat; B1, A1, A12 and A4: scarf; B1, B11, A1 and A12: present; B1, B4, A1 and A4: bow; B8, B3, A19 and A17: sleigh and rope; B2 and A3: eyes; B10, A11 and A17: nose; B3 and A17: stones of mouth; B7, B6, A15 and A16: green of trees; B10 and A10: walls of house; B4 and A4: window frames; B6, A16 and A3: doors; B3 and A17: little piece of roof.

Dorsing
Dorso blue (assort. 1): sky behind house.

Perforating (shallow)
With 3-needle tool and Semi-Star perforating tool according to pattern.

FRONTPAGE

INSERT

Enlarge 200%

Tracing
Tinta white (01T): stripes between and on Semi-Star perforations (see color example).

Embossing
Line around opening, eyes, stones of mouth, window frames, doors, rope and between 3-needle perforations according to pattern. Very lightly between double lines of outline, carrot, scarf, bow, sleigh and trees. With Hockey Stick embossing tool and Extra Large Ball embossing tool: snowman, hat, roof, house, present and snow.

Perforating (deep)
With 3-needle tool and Semi-Star perforating tool according to pattern.

SNOWMAN

General
The inner card is made of ordinary parchment paper and the outer card is made of blue Fantasy Parchment (art.no. 1476).

Tracing
Tinta turquoise (05T): snowman, snow; Tinta sepia (12T): broomstick, broom, eyes, mouth, buttons, fence; Tinta orange (06T): hat, scarf, nose; Tinta Pearl white (01TP): double lines of center border, designs in corners on cover; Tinta Pearl blue (02TP): double lines of card outline.

Painting
Tinta Pearl white (01TP) + little dab of Tinta Pearl blue (02TP): snowman, snow; Tinta Pearl white (01TP) + dab of Tinta orange (06T): hat, scarf, nose; Tinta Pearl yellow (16TP): (lines of) broom; Tinta Pearl sepia (12TP): fence, eyes, mouth, buttons, shapes on scarf + fringe, broomstick, (lines of) broom; Tinta Pearl white (01TP): between double lines of center border and card outline.

Perforating (shallow)
With Cross-Shape perforating tool according to pattern.

Embossing
Snowman, hat, scarf, broomstick, (lines of) broom,

Stippling
With 1-needle tool between double lines of outline and all lines between and on Semi-Star perforations.

Cutting
Cut out 3-needle perforations of opening.

Finishing
Fold the card. Attach the insert sheet in the card with double-sided tape. Perforate with the 2-needle tool along the card outline and cut these perforations out.

Enlarge 200%

between Cross-shape perforations according to pattern, between double lines of center border and card outline.
With Star Tool embossing tool according to pattern.

Perforating (deep)
With Cross-Shape perforating tool according to pattern.

Finishing
Perforate with the 2-needle tool along the center border and cut these perforations out. Perforate with the 4-needle tool along the card outline and cut out the outer perforations. Fold the inner card and the outer card. Attach the inner card in the outer card with double-sided tape. Cut the inner card and the back sheet of the outer card off straight.

NOSTALGIC CHRISTMAS CARD

General
The card and the insert sheet are made of ivory Fantasy Parchment (art.no. 1477).

Tracing
Tinta Pearl sepia (12TP): entire picture, card outline of front sheet and card outline of insert sheet.

Painting
Tinta sepia (12T): entire picture (look carefully at the color example and try to alternate dark and light as best as you can); Tinta Pearl sepia (12TP): shadow; Pintura brown (12): dots on berries and very little for darkest accents.

Perforating (shallow)
With Four in Four and Semi-Square perforating tool according to pattern.

Embroidering
Embroider using a fine needle with metallic header 142 7011 (Sulky) according to embroidery pattern.

Embossing
Lantern, bow, candle, berries, holly leaves, long leaves, ribbon under lantern, between double oval lines, four dots between embroidered parts of stars and outline.

Stippling
With the 1-needle tool between the two lines of the oval.

Perforating (deep)
With Semi-Square perforating tool according to pattern.

Finishing
Cut the front sheet off straight along the outline. With Tinta Pearl sepia (12TP), trace lines in the Semi-Square perforations on the insert sheet. Cut the back sheet out straight and fold the card. Cut the insert sheet out along the outer perforations. Attach the insert sheet to a yellow ocher sheet of ordinary paper with double-sided tape and attach the entire construction in the card.

INSERT

FRONTPAGE

BACKPAGE

Enlarge 141%